OUR SAVIOR
IS BORN

OUR SAVIOR

by Dan Carr
Illustrated by Don Kueker

Copyright © 1984 Concordia Publishing House
3558 S. Jefferson Avenue, St. Louis, MO 63118
Manufactured in the United States of America

07 08 09 10 11 12 13 14 15   05 04 03 02 01 00 99 98 97

IS BORN

Listen! Children,
Let me tell
Of God's great love
And how it fell
On Bethlehem
    one starry night.

Shepherds on the hills did stand
Watching their flocks
    graze the land
A star shone brightly in the sky
It flashed and blinked
    and stood nearby.

An angel told a message true:
A Child this night is born to you,
A tiny Child in manger bed—
God's own dear Son,
The angel said.

The shepherds ran
  with happy faces
Down the hills and to the place
Where Jesus lay on bed of hay.
A miracle they saw.

Long ago the message went forth
That to the land of their birth
Each family must go
To be counted.

So Joseph and Mary
And the donkey she rode
To Bethlehem on a dark dusty road
Set forth on their journey.

To find a room was no easy chore.
The rooms were full;
There were no more.
So a stable was found,
And there Jesus was born.

A stable's a place
Where animals stay,
A place where they eat,
A place where they lay.

A stable's the place
Where Jesus was born,
Amidst all the animals,
Who helped keep Him warm.

And over the stable
A bright star appeared
That gave a heavenly light.
It's beautiful message was loud and clear:
A Savior is born this night.

In a land far away
Wise Men from the east
Began to ride toward the star.
To find this Child, this Son of God
They rode their camels far.

A long long journey they did have
To reach His manger bed.
The gifts they brought were for a king,
"The King of kings," they said.

A little Child is born this night
To change the world, to bring it light.
A Child is born, so meek and mild,
God's only Son, God's lovely Child.

So join me, children, as we sing
Our happy joyful songs.
A Child is born, our Lord and King;
He came to right our wrongs.

Love came down at Christmas
Is the song that we sing,
And Jesus to Your manger
All our love we bring.

Yes, listen, children,
Let me tell
Of God's great love
And how it fell
On Bethlehem one starry night

Away in

American, 19th cent.

1 A - way in a man - ger, no crib for his bed, The lit - tle Lord
2 The cat - tle are low - ing; the poor ba - by wakes, But lit - tle Lord
3 Be near me, Lord Je - sus; I ask you to stay Close by me for -

Je - sus laid down his sweet head; The stars in the sky ___ looked
Je - sus no cry - ing he makes. I love you, Lord Je - sus; look
ev - er and love me, I pray. Bless all the dear chil - dren in

down where he lay, The lit - tle Lord Je - sus a - sleep on the hay.
down from the sky, And stay by my cra - dle till morn - ing is nigh.
your ten - der care And fit us for heav - en to live with you there.

a Manger

ilent Night

Joseph Mohr, 1792-1848

Franz Gruber, 1787-1863

1 Si - lent night, ho - ly night! All is calm, all is bright Round yon
2 Si - lent night, ho - ly night! Shep-herds quake at the sight; Glo - ries
3 Si - lent night, ho - ly night! Son of God, love's pure light Ra - diant

vir - gin moth - er and child. Ho - ly In - fant, so ten - der and mild,
stream from heav - en a - far, Heav'n-ly hosts sing, Al - le - lu - ia!
beams from your ho - ly face With the dawn of re - deem - ing grace,

Sleep in heav - en - ly peace, Sleep in heav - en - ly peace.
Christ, the Sav - ior, is born! Christ, the Sav - ior, is born!
Je - sus, Lord, at your birth, Je - sus, Lord, at your birth.